REFLECTIVE WRITING

POCKET STUDY SKILLS

Series Editor: ***Kate Williams****, Oxford Brookes University, UK*
Illustrations by Sallie Godwin

For the time-pushed student, the *Pocket Study Skills* pack a lot of advice into a little book. Each guide focuses on a single crucial aspect of study giving you step-by-step guidance, handy tips and clear advice on how to approach the important areas which will continually be at the core of your studies.

Published

14 Days to Exam Success
Blogs, Wikis, Podcasts and More
Brilliant Writing Tips for Students
Completing Your PhD
Doing Research
Getting Critical
Planning Your Essay
Planning Your PhD
Reading and Making Notes
Referencing and Understanding Plagiarism
Reflective Writing
Report Writing
Science Study Skills
Studying with Dyslexia
Success in Groupwork
Time Management
Writing for University

Pocket Study Skills
Series Standing Order
ISBN 978–0230–21605–1
(outside North America only)

You can receive future titles in this series as they are published by placing a standing order. Please contact your bookseller or, in case of difficulty, write to us at the address below with your name and address, the title of the series and the ISBN quoted above.

Customer Services Department,
Macmillan Distribution Ltd, Houndmills,
Basingstoke, Hampshire RG21 6XS
England

REFLECTIVE WRITING

POCKET STUDY SKILLS

Kate Williams, Mary Woolliams
and Jane Spiro

macmillan education palgrave

First published 2012 by
PALGRAVE MACMILLAN

Palgrave Macmillan in the UK is an imprint of Macmillan Publishers Limited, registered in England, company number 785998, of 4 Crinan Street, London N1 9XW.

Palgrave Macmillan in the US is a division of St Martin's Press LLC,
175 Fifth Avenue, New York, NY 10010.

Palgrave Macmillan is the global academic imprint of the above companies and has companies and representatives throughout the world.

Palgrave® and Macmillan® are registered trademarks in the United States, the United Kingdom, Europe and other countries

ISBN: 978-0-230-37725-7

This book is printed on paper suitable for recycling and made from fully managed and sustained forest sources. Logging, pulping and manufacturing processes are expected to conform to the environmental regulations of the country of origin.

A catalogue record for this book is available from the British Library.

A catalog record for this book is available from the Library of Congress.

Printed and bound by CPI Group (UK) Ltd, Croydon, CR0 4YY

Contents

Acknowledgements

Many people have contributed to this guide and we would like to thank them all. The experiences and puzzlement of students we have worked with was our starting point, and through them we learnt about the particular challenges of reflective writing. We are particularly grateful to students whose extracts appear in this book and bring it to life.

We have also drawn on many conversations with staff, both in the text and in the comments captured in the margins. Many thanks to all who have contributed their thoughts from inception to critical review:

Colleagues at Oxford Brookes University, UK: Dan Ferret, Lorna Froud, Jo Moyles, Mark Turnbull (Careers Centre); Annie Cripps, Anna Klenert and Angie Maher (Business and Hospitality); Alison Honour (Creative Arts); Andrew Rendell (Life Sciences); Sally Richards (Social Work); Catherine Gilson, Jean Clark and Helen Wilson, Paul Wickens and Nick Swarbrick (Education). Jane Penty (lecturer in Product Design, Central St Martins College, London). Michelle Reid (Study Adviser, Reading University, UK).

Thanks too to Sallie Godwin for her inventive and astute illustrations, and to Suzannah Burywood and colleagues in the editing and production teams at Palgrave Macmillan who have been endlessly supportive and creative in making this book happen.

Introduction

Guidance for written tasks set at university or college often expect you to show that you can 'reflect' and that your work will be 'reflective':

Write a reflective commentary on …
Give a reflective account of …
Write a reflective essay on …

Other written tasks do not explicitly ask for 'reflection' but your lecturers (or assessors) may nonetheless expect it. You might get comments like this:

I am not sure what your comments mean for you in practice ...

Your comments on your reading are rather descriptive. You need to be more reflective ...

This looks like an emotional response without any evidence of a search through the literature ...

Is this just your opinion?

This can leave students feeling uncertain about what is expected:

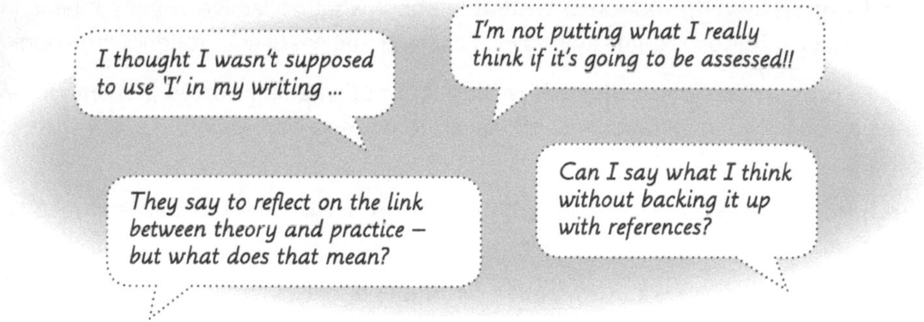
I thought I wasn't supposed to use 'I' in my writing ...
I'm not putting what I really think if it's going to be assessed!!
They say to reflect on the link between theory and practice – but what does that mean?
Can I say what I think without backing it up with references?

This guide has been written to show students:

- what 'reflection' means in different contexts in university or college
- how to bring a 'reflective' dimension into your writing.

About this book

Part 1 Understanding reflective writing is about what 'reflective writing' means in practice, and introduces some key ways of thinking that are used throughout the book.

Part 2 Form and style in reflective writing looks at what is involved in many of the forms of reflective writing students are asked to do, and considers how your work is assessed.

Part 3 Reflection in reading and writing is about making the link between reading and practice – and how you show this in your writing.

Part 4 Using frameworks in reflective writing is about different models or 'frameworks' for a structured piece of reflective writing. It includes an extended example using the Gibbs reflective cycle.

Part 5 Reflection for career planning invites you to use the habit of reflection in planning your next steps – to persuade an employer that you are the person they are looking for.

PART 1

UNDERSTANDING REFLECTIVE WRITING

Part 1 starts to unpack what is meant by 'reflection' and 'reflective writing': what it is, why you are asked to write in this way, and, of course, HOW to approach it.

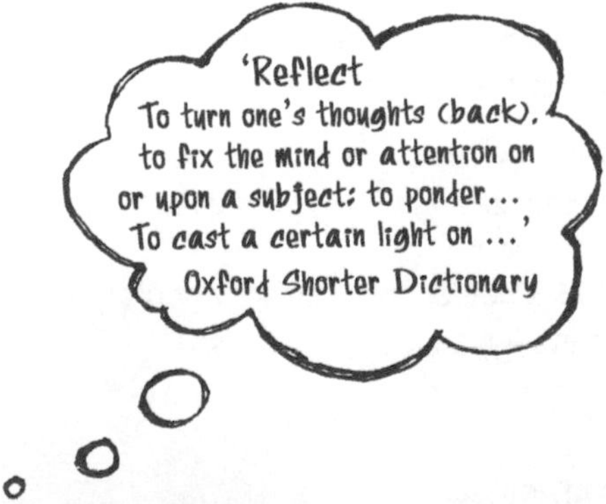
'Reflect
To turn one's thoughts (back), to fix the mind or attention on or upon a subject: to ponder...
To cast a certain light on ...'
Oxford Shorter Dictionary

1 About reflection

Reflection starts with thinking about something. As Jenny Moon (2005 p1) observes, we don't reflect on 'simple' things like the route to the corner shop, but on 'things for which there is not an obvious or immediate solution'.

You could say that reflection is not about what you're going to have for dinner this evening as you whizz round the shops. But it could be. If you are thinking about who will be eating it, what happened last time … then something apparently as simple as a shopping list could involve a lot of reflection.

It is not just to do with the subject matter of **what** you are thinking about or learning, but **how** you think about it and how you learn.

Being reflective involves being:

- **open** to different ideas, seeing things from different angles
- **curious** – asking questions
- **patient** – if the issue is not 'simple' the answer probably isn't either (though it can suddenly jump out at you)

- **honest** with yourself, your uncertainties, what you're getting wrong – or right – and your writing needs to make this **transparent** to others, so they can see it too
- **rigorous** – being analytical, and acting on the insights you gain.

Reflection in a programme of study or professional context is a purposeful activity. It drives learning and change and it's probably fair to say that no one finds change easy. Purposeful reflection can change how we think about things, what we do and how we do it, and can lead to specific changes in planning for what we do next.

Turn the page to see some of the **outcomes** of the reflections on a group task of some Product Design students, in response to the prompt:

> *If I did this project over again I would …*

By looking back on their experience and reflecting on it, these students have learnt a lot in a short period of time about working with others – and you as a reader can see this. The process by which these 'learning outcomes' were reached was rather more complex, individual and, for the students, often uncomfortable … as you'll see.

This example illustrates why tutors on so many courses include tasks that involve reflection. They want you to experience this deeper kind of learning, to engage in creative problem solving – and they want to see evidence of it in your writing.

Start by introducing ourselves and getting everyone to say what they are good at.
Work at a faster pace and multitask.
Construct a timetable for the group so as not to waste time.
Be a bit more assertive in the discussions and when tasks are handed out.
Give more feedback on other people's ideas early on.
Try to speak more even if we do not know each other well.
Figure out exactly how it might work before investing in any materials.
Split into smaller groups with specific roles.

2 Getting started on reflective writing

'Reflective' writing is new to most people. The comments below point to the confusions around what reflective writing is when it is part of a course or programme, which, of course, is assessed in some way or another:

For students who have never experienced reflective practice, it is hard to see the experience in a personal and analytical way. (Lecturer, Product Design)

- *'I thought I wasn't supposed to use "I" in my writing …'*
- *'I'm not putting what I really think if it's going to be assessed!!'*
- *'They say to reflect on the link between theory and practice – but what does that mean?'*
- *'Can I say what I think without backing it up with references?'*

You can see the tension, the opposite pulls, in reflective writing required as part of a college programme. Tutors are aware of it too, and try to resolve it in a number of ways. For example, they may:

- want to know that an informal private log or diary exists, that you add to it regularly, but they do not directly assess the contents

- ask you to respond to specific questions that draw on your 'private' record or recollections
- ask you to select incidents or experiences from your private records, and to write about them to show how they have contributed to your learning. Your writing is personal, but not private.

'Reflection' means different things in different disciplines

In all subjects you need to think reflectively about what you learn. Part of your training as a student is to draw you into the specific ways of thinking in your discipline:

... trying to make a connection between what was up on the board or in the notes, and something that I actually experienced in real life (p59).[1] *(Electronic Engineering student)*

A good healthy dose of cynicism – keep your mind open in case new data comes in (p60). (Biological Sciences lecturer)

... weigh different situations and find a middle road ... you're having to account to things that the theory hasn't accounted for (p62). (Economics lecturer)

The first fundamental thing to grasp is that all is not what it seems to be (p63). (Media and Communications student)

We expect students to develop personal skills of analysis independent of other critical authorities. (English Literature lecturer)

Reflection isn't navel-gazing. It's about moving on to an outcome. (Hospitality lecturer)

We show how our ideas develop – why we did it, what we meant by it, who influenced us, how we changed things. (Creative Arts student)

It's a way of helping us to make sense of our experiences, linking to theory and research, to help us develop our practice ... (Health and Social Care student)

We have to say what we have learnt about our own practice as a teacher and what we are doing to do to improve the way we teach. (Education student)

You've got to know yourself. You can't apply for a job unless you do. (Careers adviser)

1 The source for the comments with page numbers is Entwistle (2009).

The common thread that runs through all these is the whirring sound of thinking: stepping back to think is a conscious and deliberate process.

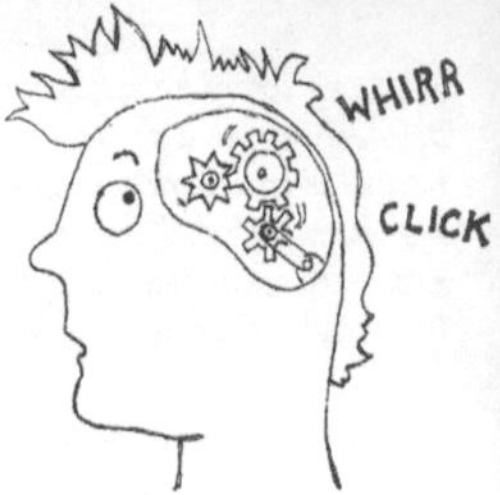

Reflective writing tasks are different too

You may also be required to demonstrate reflection in specific writing tasks, or in a 'reflective' style of writing. These too will differ from subject to subject – both in the content (what you write about) and in the process (how you write). The first step is to look at what you have been asked to do.

The task: how is it described?

Tutors set tasks that are tailored to the needs and practices of the particular discipline you are studying. They are described in a variety of ways:

Diary Journal Learning log Reading log
e-Portfolio Reading portfolio Log book
Research log Field log Design report
Critical incident report Work placement diary
Practice portfolio Reflective essay

The emphasis will differ from one course to another, but in all these forms of writing you are likely to include an element of reflection on:

- yourself
- how you learn
- how you learn from what you have done, thought, experienced, created
- how your knowledge and understanding have developed through your reading
- how you link theory and practice
- how your learning shapes further learning, your practice, work placement or employment.

In short, your writing will be about how you, your understanding and your skills develop and change over time.

The task you have been set will have a particular focus – look closely at the guidance you have been given.

What guidance have you been given?

You will often be given headings or questions to guide you as to what you are expected to write *about* and how you should *structure* your work.

For example

Diary: six diary entries

The diary will be based on a series of questions and discussion points introduced in class and developed through reflection, assignments and discussion with class peers.

Each entry should be about 250 words.

Diary entry 1

- Are there any patterns in the way I work as a learner in classes at school/college/university?
- What approaches and methods work best for me?
- What approaches and methods work least well?
- How might this understanding help me as a teacher?

Advanced Methodology of Foreign Language Teaching, undergraduate

This gives you the content and structure. Now look further through your course materials to see **how the task is assessed**. For the task above this includes:

- Demonstrating awareness of the connections between your own learning experiences and the practice and principles of good teaching.

This gives you some really useful guidance. The task is an invitation to reflect on how you learn, but it isn't enough to describe or 'tell the story' of your learning. You must also show that you can pick out what you have learnt from the classes and your reading, and that you are reflecting on how you might *apply* this learning to your eventual practice.

3 Reflective and critical writing

The words 'critical' and 'reflective' are often used in the same assignment brief.

For example

> **The task:** A reflective journal to include an analysis of your approach to …
>
> **Learning outcomes assessed**
>
> Having completed this module successfully students will be able to:
>
> i evaluate and reflect upon their own learning
>
> ii develop critical and analytical thinking skills
>
> iii …

The terms 'critical' and 'reflective' may be combined in the instruction to 'reflect critically' on something. Both terms describe a quality in writing where the reader can see that the writing comes from careful thinking.

To be critical you step up from *description* to *analysis* and move up the 'stairway' of critical thinking. You weigh up the merits or usefulness of an idea or approach (*evaluate*), use ideas or approaches in your work (*apply*), and *justify* why you adopted this approach and not that approach. These are the qualities your tutor or instructor is looking for and these are the qualities that attract the higher grades.

The stairway to critical thinking

	Justify	Use critical thinking to develop arguments, draw conclusions, make inferences and identify implications.
	Apply	Transfer the understanding you have gained from your critical evaluation and use in response to questions, assignments and projects.
	Evaluate	Assess the worth of an idea in terms of its relevance to your needs, the evidence on which it is based and how it relates to other pertinent ideas.
	Synthesise	Bring together different sources of information to serve an argument or idea you are constructing. Make logical connections between the different sources that help you shape and support your ideas.
	Compare	Explore the similarities, differences between the ideas you are reading about
	Analyse	Examine how these key components fit together and relate to each other.
Describe	**Understand**	Comprehend the key points, assumptions, arguments and evidence presented.
	Process	Take in the information i.e. what you have read, heard, seen or done.

Source: Williams (2009). For more on the stairway, see *Getting Critical* p. 13 in this series.

Good reflective writing shows the same qualities as good 'critical' writing, with two key differences. In reflective writing:

1 You and your thinking are more visible in your writing.
2 Your personal journey – what you have done, thought and read, the changes you make along the way, and what you will do next – is part of the subject of your writing.

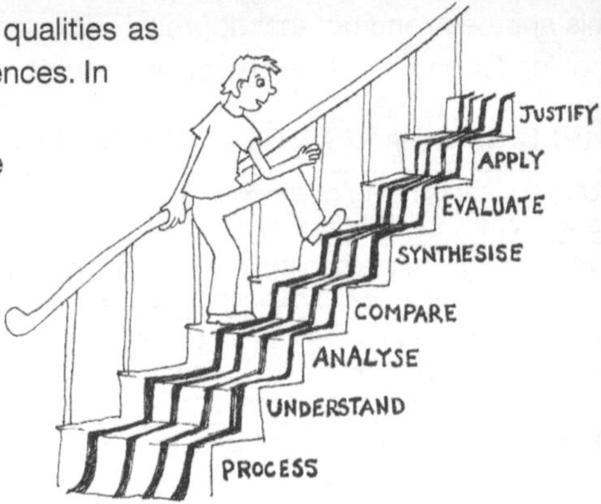

Writing focus: what does reflective writing look like?

Reflective writing will have two key elements:

1 **Using 'I':** you are writing about yourself: *I*, *my*, *me*, *mine* (the first person) and your feelings, actions, values, thoughts, practice.
2 **Looking back:** you are likely to be looking back and reflecting on how your ideas or approach has changed – what happened **then**, and your analysis and reflections on it **now**.

Using 'I' I felt … I was … I am disappointed in myself… my actions …	… it became apparent to me that there had been a clear breakdown in communication. At the time I felt disappointed that such a simple yet important task could not be carried out correctly. I was demoralised further by the fact that there was no way of rectifying the problem in time. Looking back on this experience now, I am thoroughly disappointed in myself … Ultimately it was my responsibility … On further reflection, this experience highlights a series of faults in my actions … I realise now that I should have …	**Looking back** **Then** At the time … looking back … a series of faults **And now** I am disappointed in myself … this highlights … I realise now

Benjamin Preece (Business and Hospitality student) work placement portfolio (see pp. 42–4).

4 Asking strategic questions

The six strategic questions[2] used by many people to get started on tackling a task are just as useful in relation to your reflective writing task. Read your course materials carefully, and check online to make sure you have all the information available. Lecturers will of course assume you have read it all!

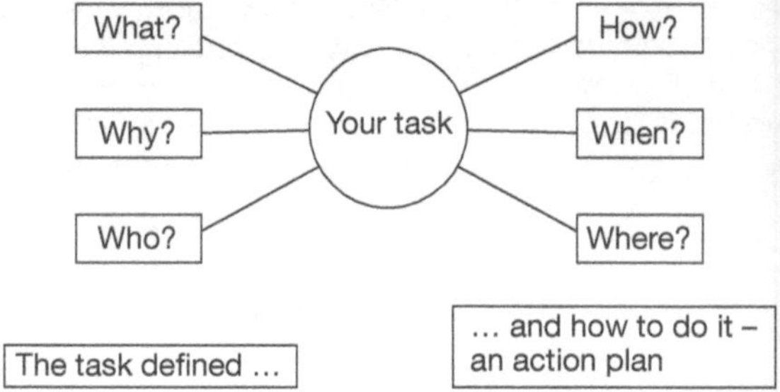

What exactly do you have to DO in your reflective task? The task defined …

Try asking yourself the first three strategic questions, using the prompts below.

---

2 This framework is also used in *Getting Critical* (pp. 1–6) and *Time Management* (pp. 39–43) in this series.

What ... exactly are you being asked to produce?	
What format? Regular entries? Different items for a portfolio?	
Any guidance about structure, layout, style, presentation?	
How long/number of words?	
What % of the overall course mark is it worth?	

Why ... are you being asked to write 'reflectively'?	
To focus on your learning? Where is this explained most clearly?	
To help you achieve specific learning outcomes? What are they?	

Who ... are you writing for? It is crucial to be clear about your reader and what they are looking for in your writing	
Yourself – you and only you will read this private learning diary?	
Others – e.g. your tutor, placement mentor, potential employer? What do they want to see in it?	

When you are clear in your own mind about the answers to the first three strategic questions, you can see what you are expected to do.

You may also have found yourself moving beyond the specific questions to the big, overarching question:

So ... what are the implications ...
... for how I see things? ... for me as a developing practitioner?
... for how I write? ... for the incidents I choose?

Getting it done – an action plan

Take a few more moments to work through the last three strategic questions – the ones that will help you clarify the practicalities of the task you have been set.

How ... do you write?	
Your aim is to match the style of writing the tutor expects in a good assignment. What guidance do you have on this? Are you clear about the answers to the frequently asked questions on p. ix?	

When ... is the deadline for the final hand-in?	
Are there earlier deadlines, e.g. for individual entries/posts?	
Will you write before a key event? Immediately after? Some time later?	

Where ...? will you do your writing?	
You decide and make the time and space for it ...	

If, after working through your course materials and answering the six strategic questions, you are still not clear, or you find some information gaps, ASK! The tutor may welcome the opportunity to clarify points of potential confusion for the wider group of students.

What next?

This question – another big one – moves you on to action: getting started.

PART 2

FORM AND STYLE IN REFLECTIVE WRITING

Part 2 considers many of the forms of writing in which you may be asked to record or draw on your reflections.

It starts with immediate reactions to an event, and ends with forms of writing and thinking that develop over time.

ary Journal Learning log Reading lo
Portfolio Reading portfolio Log book
esearch log Field log Design repo
itical incident report Work placement di

5 Reflecting on yourself and your experiences

You and your thoughts and experiences are the starting points for reflective writing.

Something happens ...

A group of first year Product Design students meet for the first time to work in a large team ...

This, of course, is mind reading – an impossibility! Any written account of an experience comes after, and will be edited in some way. That said, the sooner you make notes or write down your experiences, the better you will remember not only what happened, but your feelings at the time. All this contributes to your reflections, whatever form they take.

What happened?

Very quickly you look back on an experience, and when you talk or write about it you are able to see the sequence of events, your role and feelings. You begin to *analyse* what was going on. Below are some of the written comments the students made soon after the short group project was completed, in response to the question:

> *What was the most challenging aspect of the project for you personally?*

Rather than trying not to think about the experience (which many people do with an experience they'd prefer to forget!), these students have had concentrate on it and *analyse* their reactions.

I found it was difficult to get a message across ...

Working with new classmates ... we didn't know each other and didn't know what each one was good at ...

... a group of people formed the core of the group and dominated decision making ... I had to fight my way ...

... the language barrier ... the others might not understand what I was saying ... I felt a bit brushed off ...

... trying to take a leading role without looking like a control freak ...

... I know that a quiet person can have an idea or opinion which is just as good as those of an outspoken one ...

... I come from another language and culture ... So there was an invisible gap amongst all of us ...

... trying to take an important role ... it was all too easy to let others get on with it ...

Reflecting on how you learn

In the comments below you can see how each writer analyses their experience of learning, and shows self-knowledge in their reflection:

- *'I have been a last-minute person since school years and it has extended into university years. I feel more motivated when I am doing my work at the very last minute …* (Education student)
- *'I found the exercises required me to think in ways I wouldn't necessarily do naturally …'* (Medical student)
- *'My brain is splitting with trying to learn so much in such a short space. Working in the hotel is so different from what I imagined …'* (Business and Hospitality student)
- *'I love the rush of idea generation, sketch development and the tension of the process …'* (Creative Arts student)

These kinds of comments may form part of a reflective journal, in which the writer looks back at past experiences to inform future development:

> When I was at school, there was not a strong emphasis on learning another language. English was/is seen as the key language to the world … I feel a lot of my resistance to learning another language has been influenced by this attitude … and attending lessons was a chore I didn't want to do …

As an adult, I can see how many of the lessons were uninspiring and I had no reason to believe that learning would be to my advantage …

As a teacher I hope to be able to …

Advanced Methodology of Foreign Language Teaching, undergraduate

Writing focus: describing when – past, present and future

Look at how the examples above move between the past, the present and the future – spontaneously reflected in the verbs the writers use.

Verbs describing **past time** are used to recount events or experiences that happened in the past:
When I was … I didn't want to…
I found … I was able to … I felt …

Verbs describing **present time** are used for things that are true now – current thoughts or feelings or present reflections arising from past experiences:
I can see now why … I like … I don't think …
I find that … I feel … I tend to … I like to consider …

And looking ahead to the **future**
I hope to be able to … I'd like to …

6 Finding your voice

Since the focus of reflective writing is you, your thoughts and development, your readers want to hear your 'voice'. Students sometimes feel that under the weight of all the reading they have to do – commenting on what this writer said and how it's different from that writer's opinion – that their own voice isn't right, or isn't good enough. Wrong. It's always you who's writing, not a machine or some ideal-type student, and your reader wants a sense of who you are – particularly in reflective writing.

Online discussions

These can be especially good for finding your voice as you can post your reactions immediately after (or in the case of tweeting, during) an event. You're not sending your thoughts off into a void, but into conversation with other – possibly many other – people. Here are some comments from students joining an online discussion:

'I can't believe it's only a week since I first logged on ... It's become addictive ...'

'I really like blogging – not sure why it's different from writing a journal but it just is ...'

> 'I don't leave enough time to think before I post – but then I don't think before I speak very much either.'

> 'I like learning new things – you learn something new every time you log on – get that lovely rush and tempted to do more ...'

You can hear the person talking here: they really do have a 'voice'. They aren't presenting a tidied-up finished product, but talking about the process they are involved in. They all show a self-awareness and excitement about this new form of learning. Keeping your 'voice' in all your writing is key to good writing, and especially in reflective writing.

Think for a moment about the particular opportunities and risks of online communication. Conversations online do not have the verbal cues and body language of face-to-face communication, so think particularly carefully about the words you use in online discussions, blogs, posts, texts and email.

Before you hit 'Send', take a split second to reflect whether you've got the right balance between:

- the urgency of what you want to say … and
- the more considered view you might later wish you'd taken …

– remembering the other people who will be party to your comments…

… and the risk of alienating your online community.

Kathleen Yancey (1998 p11) puts this more elegantly: 'we learn to understand ourselves through explaining ourselves to others'. Do take the time to explain, not just react.

Writing focus: netiquette

Online discussion forums as part of your course are … well … part of your course! So they are different to tweeting or texting on anything you fancy. Make sure you are clear about:

- **why** the forum has been set up, the aims of the discussion: purely social? Support by sharing experiences? Ideas or thoughts on reading or an activity? For sharing assessed work on (e.g.) reading?
- **who** will be reading what you write: the tutor? Other students? A wider group?
- **what** you should write about: are there some experiences you should/should not share here?

and reflect on **how**, as a consequence, you should write.

The virtual environment has its own potential pitfalls. Without being able to see the people in your conversations you don't get the verbal clues and immediate feedback as you talk, so it's harder to judge if you're getting the tone right …

Jenni: Hi guys, I'm thinking about focusing my reflections on our decision not to nominate a leader for our team … What do you think?

Fas: Hi Jenni, Personally I'm convinced that leadership is essential in teams – I think we would have achieved a higher standard in our project if we had decided on a leader at the beginning. What do the rest of you think?

Justin: What planet are you on, Fas? A team leader isn't essential, and can be destructive to team processes … End of.

Whoops Justin! Count to 5 and start again!

Fas makes it clear he is speaking for himself.

He invites other viewpoints.

This comes across as aggressive. Justin may intend this to be light-hearted but Fas won't know this.

Justin leaves no room for debate – others may feel uncomfortable about challenging him too.

Take 2

Justin: Fas, I'm interested by your thoughts– I'd like to know more about your experiences of leadership in teams. I feel that our approach worked well, and that we may have been less effective with a leader… Thoughts anyone?

More respectful, less offputting.

Inviting others to join the debate ...

Depending on the purpose of the discussion forum, you may be expected to link your experiences to theory in your reflections (see pp. 56–9):

Take 3

Justin: [... we may have been less effective with a leader.] In some circumstances teams do better without a leader ... That article by Barker (2004) did make me think that ...

Referring out to evidence for views can not only cool passionately held views, but direct the discussion towards evidence and away from personal beliefs – and heated language.

Do keep your voice, but make sure you take that split second to stop, reflect ... and edit your comments for a constructive discussion!

'I like to consider posts from others and to frame my responses before posting' (extract from student post).
Wise words.

7 A reflective diary or learning journal

Students across a range of disciplines are often asked to keep a reflective diary, portfolio or journal. This is not really surprising since a diary/log/journal is a record of your development as a learner or practitioner in your field. Exactly what goes in your journal will, of course, vary from one discipline to another.

Learning journal in creative subjects

Students learning to create or build something – a bridge (Engineering), a product (Product Design), a structure (Architecture), an artwork (Creative Arts) – will be learning to:

- **look at** or **observe** objects, paintings, structures
- **analyse** what they see (form, function, materials)
- **consider** how each element contributes to the whole
- **be aware of** how they have **borrowed, changed** or **built on** the ideas of other practitioners, artists or theories
- **reflect** on their own **developmental process**: starting, experimenting, changing, adapting, starting again.

This development of ideas is likely to be recorded in a personal **record** or sketchbook. Often it is only later that you can see the origins of the ideas you work on. You don't see it at the time, which, of course, underlines the importance of these informal records not only for students in these disciplines but for everyone who wants or needs to chart their development. Only at the end of the process do you see the path to the outcome clearly.

You can then write a summative piece that explains and justifies the choices you made along the way:

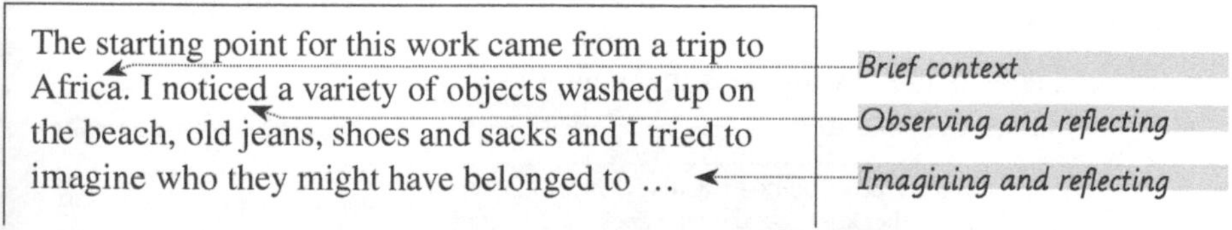

The starting point for this work came from a trip to Africa. I noticed a variety of objects washed up on the beach, old jeans, shoes and sacks and I tried to imagine who they might have belonged to …
Brief context
Observing and reflecting
Imagining and reflecting

… I looked at Marcel Duchamp, Christian Boltanski and Bill Woodrow to see how artists made use of found objects

Building on other artists' work

… I noticed that when two or three unrelated objects were placed together […] the audience would find themselves trying to identify a link between the objects …

Observing and reflecting

Awareness of audience and reflecting

I looked at ways of preserving the objects and learnt about casting and the range of materials to cast from including wax, chocolate, resin and plaster …

Experimenting

I wasn't really happy with how the wax teacup turned out … I became fascinated with shoes …

Testing … feelings and reflecting

Changing

I discovered fibreglass – the delicacy and opaqueness of the fibreglass shoe …

Experimenting … reflecting

… I hope the installation stimulates the memories and imagination of the audience.

Connecting with audience

Thanks to Pippa Chambers (Creative Arts student) for her kind permission to include this extract.

Learning journal in Health/Social Care

A Health/Social Care student will learn to:

- **participate in** or **observe** an incident (such as the care of a client)
- **discuss** what went well and not so well about it
- **analyse** their thoughts about it, by linking to relevant theory/policy/science/guidance, and to the experience of others
- **reflect** on how this links to their own experiences – how could this inform their future practice?

A junior nurse's reflective diary entry

Last week my mentor transferred a client into her bed without using any equipment to assist her. The client was unable to stand safely. However my mentor said there was no hoist nearby and it would take too much time to go and find one. Since then I have had my moving and handling training update, in which I learned about laws and policies related to moving and handling and the nurse's responsibility in relation to health and safety at work, including

Describing the incident

Observing

The incident continued. Unstated concern about poor practice

New learning on policy and guidance

the Health and Safety at Work Act (1974). I am sure that using a hoist would have reduced the risk of injury to the patient as well as to the nurse who was moving her. After my training, I feel more confident to challenge others' practice, and I realise the importance of being assertive to ensure my own safety as well as the safety of clients and colleagues.

Reflection on practices and implications

Reflection on self and future practice

A medical student reflects

[The exercise] was to consider the approaches a doctor might take with a person with a chronic illness. To be honest, I didn't want to do this, as some things were too close to the bone. I'm glad I did though as the scenario our group was given was one I had never particularly considered, and I was able to consider what [the person's] particular needs would be. I suppose it was a case of separating personal and professional attitudes …

Incident/activity

Feelings/reflections

New learning

Outcome

New learning in professional context – generalising to make the link between this experience and prior understanding of the issue (personal and professional attitudes)

8 Learning journals and assessment

The fact that your work will be assessed introduces an external dimension to your reflective writing. You are writing for an audience that is not yourself. So, as with any other writing, you need to have a clear sense of what the person reading your work is looking for.

In many subject areas, university or college is a preparation for your working life in a particular sector, and you may be writing for an imaginary audience – a client, patient or colleague. In most cases, nevertheless, your grade will be determined by your teachers. What are they looking for?

Assessing creative work

Students need to know how to assess their own creative work and appreciate others', so they need to understand the multiple viewpoints from which their work will be assessed in their working lives. This leads to assessment practices that encourage students to understand where assessment criteria come from, and to use them in self-assessment.

The sequence may be something like this:

- You have a brief: from a tutor, or from a client.
- You have to interpret it and come up with ideas for how to tackle it.
- You formulate an aim: what is the work/task designed to achieve?
- You experiment and develop …
- The execution of the project is of course what the work is!

'Good' or 'not good' are not useful judgements in creative disciplines, and can lead to subjective opinions that are difficult to evidence or challenge. The question used in assessment is

How successful/effective is this work in achieving the (agreed) aim?

You still need criteria – the specific aspects against which the work is assessed.

Self-assessment: generating criteria for creative work

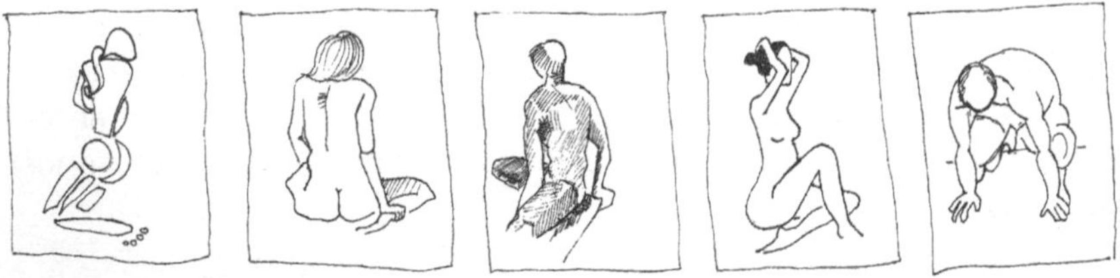

OK. Let's identify the strengths of these drawings

quality of drawn line
use of dark/light proportion
accuracy of observation gesture
atmosphere expression

These qualities can then form the basis of the assessment criteria by which work can be assessed.

Criteria	How successful is the work in achieving ...?

This approach of inviting students to identify criteria by which work is assessed can be used in other disciplines where self-assessment is required.

Being assessed – a work placement learning journal

Start with the guidance you have been given: about the purpose of the task (the **why**), **who** (exactly) will be reading it, **what** evidence they will be looking for in it, and **how** you should present it.

Check the learning outcomes (or 'syllabus', 'course content'). This is a statement of what you are expected to learn from the course or the experience. It may sound rather obvious, but your reader(s) will of course expect you to demonstrate this specific learning in your writing.

For example
The assessment criteria of a 'Professional Practice' module completed during a work placement (in Business and Hospitality) are clear about what the tutors want to see in students' reflective journals. Look closely at this guidance and pick up the clues about what you would need to show in your written work.

Knowledge and understanding

1 Analyse and evaluate specific aspects of organisational practices in the areas of operations, marketing, human resources and finance.
2 Evaluate organisational practices in relation to relevant theory and concepts in international hospitality and tourism management.

Professional skills

1 Demonstrate an ability to reflect on practical work experience drawing on relevant management theories/concepts.
2 Engage with a self-development approach to learning by identifying learning opportunities, setting and achieving learning objectives and analysing personal development.
3 Demonstrate an appreciation of diversity and cultural issues in both work and cultural groups.

You will need to have a section on each of these four. Remember your learning from the modules/courses you took before your work placement!

Link your observations about the setting you are working in to relevant theory and concepts. (Don't forget the theory just because you are on work placement.)

Link your reflections on your own experience to theory/concepts.

Use this to guide your selection of incidents from your private journal/notes.

This strongly suggests you need a structured approach.

A clear pointer – one 'learning opportunity' must be on this issue.

Here are extracts from Ben's journal entry. See how his analysis and reflection provide the evidence of knowledge, understanding and developing professional skills the tutors are looking for.

> As duty manager, I was responsible for all corporate VIP show-rounds that took place during my shift. Corporate 'show-rounds' are a key marketing tool, and before negotiations on price can begin, the hotel must impress in terms of quality of rooms and service.
>
> To prepare for an important show-round, I phoned the accommodation office with a specific set of instructions for how the suite was to be prepared … The accommodation department has 30 staff made up of over 10 different nationalities … When I conducted the show-round with the client, I entered the suite to find that none of my instructions had been carried out, resulting in a poor first impression. The show-round did not result in a booking …

Context

What happened

Looking back, I am thoroughly disappointed in myself for not ensuring that these tasks had been carried out … ultimately it was my responsibility …

Thoughts and feelings

On further reflection, this experience highlights a series of faults with my actions. As a manager in training I should have used my initiative and checked … Lashley (2000) identifies standardisation as a key hospitality retail concept whereby an organisation needs to provide an exact level of good service … Reflecting on this experience, it was clear that as a result of my failure to check […] a lack of standardisation resulted in a loss of competitive advantage, and potential clients (and revenue) were lost to competing hotels …

Analysis and reflection

Relevant theory on organisational practices

Understanding the application of concepts in practice (and consequences)

I need to develop my professional abilities … to improve my communication skills in the international working arena … and identify lines of communication that are effective and those that are not, especially in a setting with staff of

An ability to reflect on practical work experience

Setting learning objectives

so many nationalities …Hahn (2009) argues that face-to-face communication is the most effective in an international environment as it is personal and provides immediate feedback. I need to talk to colleagues …

Analyses the personal experience, gaining distance from it and new insights into it by relating it to theory.

A resolution to learn from the experience and move on – an outcome or action plan..

References

Hahn M (2009). Overcoming communication barriers in organizations. Available at http://ezinearticles.com/?Overcoming-Communication-Barriers-in-Organizations&id=1033424. [Accessed 9 June 2010]

Lashley C (2000). In search of hospitality: towards a theoretical framework. *International Journal of Hospitality Management*. 19(1) p3–15.

Thanks to Benjamin Preece (Business and Hospitality student) for his kind permission to include this extract.

Take-away points

Record incidents, thoughts, feelings – however painful! – as soon as possible after the event. By reflection you will be able to turn this into useful learning.

A little later (not so long that you have lost touch with it), be guided by the learning outcomes as you select the incidents or issues for inclusion in your more formal, assessed journal entry (such as Ben's). Check relevant theory to find out how other people have conceptualised the situation you experienced. Integrate this into your analysis of the situation, and into specific plans for your personal development. (See Part 4 for possible structures to use in a formal write-up of a journal entry.)

Your journal entry will be calm in tone and the outcome positive if you can show how you have learnt from your experiences, however stressful or negative they may have felt at the time.

9 Portfolios

A portfolio can take many forms and has many purposes. It will, of course, be set as an assessed piece of work, but it can also be a key piece of evidence for future employers. It tends to be a bulky item with all evidence of your work or experience in it. It will include reflective entries: the 'learning journal' and perhaps a longer piece of reflective writing that articulates the processes involved from start to finish. Your reader should be able to see the link between what you say you have done or learnt and the evidence that supports your claims.

Let your portfolio do the talking!

There will be things in your portfolio that mean a lot to you. Ideally, you'd talk it through with your assessor, explaining this and accounting for that. But let's assume you can't. You have to drop it off, walk away and leave it to speak for you. Whatever form it takes, do make sure it is brilliantly organised – with contents lists, colour coding, cross-references, or whatever is appropriate. You don't want to annoy your reader (or potential employer) by leaving them to muddle through your work. You want clear organisation that helps them find their way.

Try thinking of it as one half of a conversation, and imagine the questions your reader will be asking.

Your task in writing your reflective entries is to answer your reader's questions **before** they have asked them! This takes you back to:

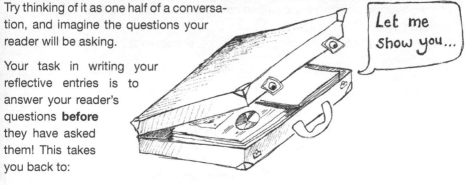

What does my reader want to see?

A work placement portfolio

The evidence in a work placement portfolio might include all or any of these:

- an outline of the setting or business you are working in
- a project, report, investigation or audit on some aspect of the running of the organisation
- assessments, self-assessments and reviews of your performance
- evidence of achievement of competencies

- specific learning objectives and written reflections on the extent to which you achieved them
- sample forms, checklists, training programmes, documentation relating to special events or procedures
- CV or personal profile
- your plans for the future.

Your reader will work through your portfolio to see how it answers their questions about what you have learnt, how you learnt it and what you will do differently next time. Your reader will be looking for a **match** between what you say and the evidence they see:

The student says ...	**The mentor/appraiser says ...**
I am enjoying my placement and am glad they believe I am doing well. I still need to work on some things …	*Yasmin is a very quick learner and takes feedback constructively to improve her performance … a very positive attitude and self-motivated. She constantly reviews her goals … Gets on brilliantly with colleagues …*

But they will be concerned by signs of a mismatch:

The student says ...	The mentor/appraiser says ...
I feel very happy with my appraisal and it is nice to see the positive feedback as I have put a lot of effort into my work.	*This ... is an area where I would like to see Michael make considerable improvement ... he would do well to seek the advice of colleagues and supervisors who have extensive first hand experience of ... and take time to listen to constructive criticism ... It's not clear to me what his development goals are ...*

The mentor, and anyone else who reads Michael's portfolio, will be concerned by his apparent lack of self-awareness, or reflection. How will this student learn if he isn't aware of the need to make changes in his approach?

A tutor might think: Why should I trust what you say? How do I know you are able to learn and improve if you say everything is perfect?! And where's the evidence?

Unreflective comments do not go down well with academic staff either:

The student says ...	The tutor suggests ...
I have demonstrated my ability to work with others in the team. I am an articulate communicator. I am able to interact effectively with other students. This was the first time I had to present with other people but I think it went very well.	*Redraft. Give an example to illustrate each point. Add how you might make the presentation even better next time.*

A reflective writer will avoid absolute judgements. They will try to balance strengths with weaknesses. The reflective writer will also give evidence or examples to explain judgements.

Take 2: what's the difference here? Look at the tutor's reactions …

The student says ...	The tutor comments ...
I felt that I engaged my audience well, and the aims of my presentation were generally met. However, there were several areas I would like to improve: firstly the amount of time I left for discussion … Secondly, I hurried my conclusion which summed up the whole point of my talk. Both of these seem to be related to my time management.	*You have been balanced and thoughtful in your account. You have both listed your key strength and identified carefully an area for development. You have given specific examples of your concerns, and recognised the common thread that connects them.*

The tutor is pleased to see signs of self-awareness and reflection – and a bit of modesty! You do yourself no favours by coming across as complacent about your performance. Everyone can identify specific areas for improvement next time around.

Students are advised to show how reflection has helped them to review and improve their practice. It may not be acceptable to show that reflection has NOT improved your practice, even if that is honest!
(Education lecturer)

10 Reflection in research

Research starts with an interest in something. When you start researching, you ask questions (about the research topic, or the research process), reflect on what you've done, and where you go next. Research is an iterative process – you go backwards and forwards, but also onwards and upwards, and reflection drives it.

Students are often required to record their progress in a work diary (in a project, dissertation or independent study module, for example). Entries are likely to show:

- what you did
- reflection, uncertainties, leading to questions
- decisions and changes in direction
- next steps.

The research spiral

Source: Reproduced from Williams et al. (2011). The co-author Clare Parfitt-Brown originally designed this model in her work with Masters students studying Dance.

7/2/12

… I have been looking through general texts in the library. I soon realised the texts would not be especially helpful as they are very broad … Nevertheless I identified useful information about the three main geo-engineering mitigation options. … I will now begin to look for journal articles, government reports and reviews to build on the information …

What you did

Reflection

Decision

Next steps

9/2/11

This afternoon I started to use electronic databases to search for relevant literature. At first I did very general searches using 'technical fixes' and 'mitigation of climate change' but I soon realised I needed to be more specific. I used 'carbon capture and storage' as a starting point and found a number of papers … I will continue to use the databases to find more sources that will form the backbone of the project.

What you did

Reflection

Change in approach

Change in outcome

Next steps

11/2/12
I had a second meeting with Dr X today. I didn't meet my target of finding the main sources I needed … I was unsure of exactly what kind of mitigation options I should be researching and whether I should focus on one country/region … In the meeting we revisited the original concept for the work, and agreed that I should be investigating the so-called 'technical fixes' … and that technology should lie at the heart of the work …

What you did

Uncertainties, questions, clarifications

Next steps

Source: From a workbook for an independent study on the technology for carbon capture, with thanks to Andrew Rendell.

Part 2 has traced a journey in the habit of reflection – from immediate reactions shortly after the event to the sort of sustained reflection you need as a researcher. You can see that reflection isn't just a one-off activity to complete a task, but can become 'a habit of mind, one that transforms' (Yancey 1998 p12).

Part 3 is about linking your reading with your practical experience and how you show this in your reflective writing.

PART 3

REFLECTION IN READING AND WRITING

Part 3 starts with showing how, through reflection, you can link personal experience with ideas, information, studies and theories you encounter in your reading.

It then takes a close look at how your reflection finds its way into your writing and ends with some specific writing tips.

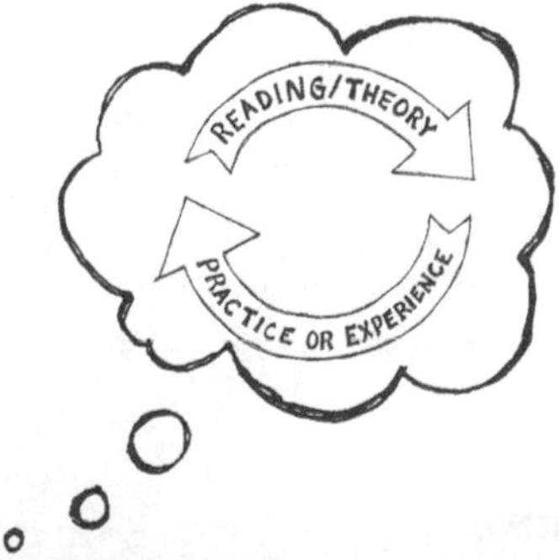

11 Linking theory and practice

The purpose of writing about what you have read is not simply to show your reader, tutor or instructor that you have done the required reading by dropping in references here and there. The purpose is to show that you can see the link between theories, ideas and approaches you read about, and their relevance to your personal experience. To do this you need first to understand the content, and then to reflect on the implications for you and your practice.

How you organize your writing can help you do this. After you have been immersed in reading, it can be tempting to keep your discussion of your reading separate from your reflections on your experience – in parallel lines that never meet, like a train track.

Instead, try making the conscious effort to reflect on the link between your experience and the theory, policies or studies you are reading.

You can then use these topic areas that link theory and practice as a basis for the paragraphs and sections in your essay or assignment.[3]

Applying what you've learnt

Being able to *apply* new ideas or information from your courses or reading is what learning is about. You become someone who can use – or reject or refute – ideas or approaches you have read about. This is why the ability to *apply* ideas is towards the

3 For more detailed suggestions on planning your work, see *Planning Your Essay*, *Getting Critical* (pp. 49–60) and *Report Writing* in this series.

top of the critical 'staircase' (p. 13), and why it is so often explicitly required for the higher grades.

To make this happen, you need to reflect on the points of connection. Your reading explains, interprets, provides evidence for, makes you rethink or resolves issues. You can draw on it or apply it to *your experience* and with it your beliefs, knowledge, values, opinions.

Whichever comes first for you – reading or experience – the point of it all is that you show that you have reflected on how the two connect. In your writing you can then discuss the implications of what you have read for what you do and how you think.

The WHO (2006) guidelines define the key moments for hand hygiene. ...

Hahn (2009) identifies face-to-face communication as the most effective in an international environment.

Effective leadership requires a confident and appropriate use of power (Barker 2004; Levin 2005).

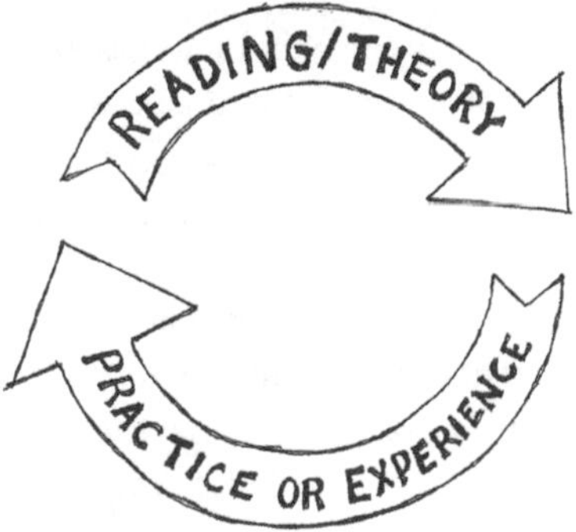

In my community placement, staff did not have access to hand-washing facilities ...

I am thoroughly disappointed in myself for not ensuring these tasks had been carried out.

Our lack of leadership resulted in meetings being overly relaxed ...

12 Writing a critical review or annotated bibliography

Writing a critical review or keeping an annotated bibliography may be set as a task by tutors for a number of reasons. It may be to encourage you to:

- become familiar with finding and using research papers
- think critically about what you've read – to take you beyond repeating back what the article says
- keep records of your research – it's surprisingly easy to forget what you've read!
- gain confidence in writing about research in your own way, in your own 'voice'.

It is also an important aid to developing the habit of reflection. The 3-point structure below – *summarise*, *evaluate*, *reflect* – helps you make the transition from understanding, to evaluating, to reflecting on its implications for you and your work.

Read your guidance carefully! It will probably tell you what the tutor is looking for and give you an indication of length. If you have no specific guidance, the structure below[4] works for both a longer critical review and a short annotation.

---

4 A short annotation in note form is shown in *Getting Critical* (p. 40) in this series.

The full reference	
Summarise What it is about? (about 25% length)	◗ The author's purpose, aim or question ◗ Main argument, central idea, findings or conclusions ◗ What sort of text is it? General? Specific?
Evaluate What do I think about it? (about 50%)	◗ Who is it written for? ◗ Particular strengths or points of interest ◗ Similarities or differences with other things you have read, or ideas you hold yourself ◗ Any weaknesses or limitations?
Reflect How might I use it? (about 25%)	Has the text helped you understand something better? Or see/do something differently? If so, what? How useful is it? If so, how?

Don't overrun on the summary and slip into describing the text. Your lecturers may well know the text already, and are interested in *your* evaluation of strengths and limitations and *your* reflections on how it relates to your thinking.

For example

> Govan P and Kuzera S (2010). Primary and secondary teachers' attributions for pupils' misbehaviour: a preliminary investigation. *Journal of Research in Special Educational Needs*. 9 (3) 51–74.

The authors' purpose was to see if contrasts in educational settings and curricular emphases might affect teachers' attributions for children's behaviour. This study is unique as there has been no systematic study of … *Overview/summary*

A key finding of this study is the contrasting views of primary and secondary teachers … *Summary moving to evaluation* The authors draw on a range of academic sources to show … *Strength identified – breadth of research* However, the authors fail to recognise the impact of the age difference … *Evaluation: limitation identified – without being negative*

The questionnaire used by the authors had been used in a pilot study … A wide range of data was collected … *Evaluation – focus on methods*

Despite the limitations, this article has many strengths …. The article is relevant to anyone interested in … and has made me more aware of … *Conclusion/reflection*

Education student (Primary Teaching)

13 That 'reflective' quality in writing

Your assessors often use assessment criteria to explain what they are looking for in your writing. The criteria for the higher grades are likely to include words and phrases explained in the 'steps' towards the upper end of the 'staircase' (p. 13):

… original interpretation …
… insightful and innovative contribution to …
…thorough and reflective data collection, analysis and interpretation …
… articulate and justify a point of view …
… analyse research findings … relate to personal experience
… excellent level of criticality …

And where is 'reflection' in these? The answer is 'everywhere', often unspoken, under-pinning these specific qualities. To achieve these higher-order qualities, you have to have a sense of curiosity, a questioning approach to practices and ideas, be open to different ideas, be honest with yourself, and rigorous and analytical in your research and actions – and show this in your writing.

Grace wrote …	The reader sees …
When placing children in ability sets following initial assessments, it is important not to assume that English as an Additional Language (EAL) learners should necessarily be in low ability groups. I found it surprising at the time that the child I observed on placement was in a high ability group since he clearly has limited language skills. I now realise that learners should be placed according to their cognitive ability across the curriculum rather than their English language skills alone, an observation that is supported by Druse and Rahill (2007). The DfES (2009) go further and suggest that learners of EAL will benefit from access to secure learners demonstrating good models of English, who are more likely to be found in higher ability groups.	A *clear voice* and clear argument, expressed in this first (topic) sentence. The paragraph provides the evidence for this argument. *Observation* and first reactions. *Reflection* – leading to … a later (and fuller) understanding of one situation from which Grace is able to generalise and bring this understanding to her future practice as a teacher … Something she observed herself … reflected on and confirmed through her reading, which moved her thinking on … and links back to the discussion about 'ability groups' in the first sentence. It's a well-written paragraph – by a reflective practitioner.

Essay: Researching effective practice (Education).

Above all, this paragraph is transparent: as a reader you can see Grace observing, puzzling, reading, reflecting some more, and coming up with some guiding principles for her future practice. The process of reflection brings about a constructive outcome – personal growth, change and new perspectives.

In science and social science reflection is present in every stage of an inquiry, especially in the methodology. Here you describe what you did, why you did it that way, and the strengths and limitations of the choices you made. The underpinning idea is that your reader should be able to replicate the process for themselves – and for this they need to understand not only what you did, but why you did it and why you made changes. Your reflections on these issues underpin your writing whatever the writing style.

Writing conventions differ from subject to subject and within disciplines. In some science and social science writing the process of reflection is masked by the objective style of writing, using the passive ('focus group interviews were conducted ...') and keeping the first person ('I') out of the writing.

Sometimes a more personal and reflective style of writing is valued:

Robbie wrote ...	The reader sees ...
Initially I conducted focus group interviews in order to gain insights and information from Village Health Workers (VHWs) regarding the issues facing their patients with HIV/AIDS. I felt the focus group structure was appropriate as it allowed many issues to be discussed by many people in a 'conversational and fluid' way (as recommended by Hills and Murphy 1997 p45) …	A clear and transparent process: a student researcher making what seems like a sensible choice about methods … which link to the aims of his research … and his reading and research into methods … *[Off-stage, Robbie observes something isn't right … puzzles … reflects …]*
[Later] I found that the VHWs were concerned with professional issues of confidentiality of the client … I decided to change the style to individual interviews … Many more details of the challenges faced by their clients were discussed with me using this method …	… and realises he is missing something. He decides to change his approach … and reflects on the difference in the data this change produces …

Thanks to Robbie Georgiou (Geography and Development Studies) for his kind permission to include this extract from his dissertation.

The extracts above show how good reflective writing is necessarily personal – you write as 'I':

Coventry University

London

Tel 024 7765 1016

Borrowed Items 02/03/2020 12:56

XXXXXX2818

Item Title	Due Date
48001000098113	23/03/2020
* Reflective writing	
48001000006520	05/03/2020
Fashion branding unraveled	
48001000060121	09/03/2020
The fashion dictionary : a visual resource for terms, techniques and styles	

* Indicates items borrowed today

Thankyou for using this unit

www.coventry.ac.uk

I found it surprising at the time … I now realize …

I felt the focus group structure was appropriate … [Later] I found that the VHWs were concerned …

Both these writers use their personal observations as a starting point, and draw confidently on their reading to add to their understanding. They don't need to say 'I think' or 'I believe' for the reader to see their reflective style of thinking at work in their writing.

Writing focus: Is it OK to write *I think* or *I believe*?

I think and *I believe* should be used sparingly and carefully – even in reflective writing.

If you overuse them a reader might think you lack:

- awareness of other practitioners or readings
- criticality: have you thought about it? questioned it?
- rigour: have you checked it is well founded?

Or you could come across as arrogant – an idea is right simply because you believe it to be!

However it IS useful when you are describing your own actions, decisions or responses:

I think I'll try a different approach next time.

Students often write *I think* or *I believe* to express an opinion on something debated in the discipline:

I believe that …	playtime is just as important for a child's school experience as class time.
I think …	a team leader is not necessary for successful group work.
In my opinion …	lack of exercise is the major cause of obesity in children.

What happens if you take off *I think* or *I believe?* You now have an opinion, no doubt sincerely held, but as it stands, without any reference to research or any other evidence, it is simply … an opinion.

Anyone can have a sincerely held opinion or belief about anything.

The statements above are perfectly sensible opinions, most likely based on personal experience and observation. They are also complex issues on which there is extensive research and much debate. Your task in reflective writing is to use your personal experience as a springboard for going deeper into an issue and researching it. Your initial opinion may be confirmed or modified as a result of your

research, but your reader will see what it is based on. It must be a reasoned, evidenced argument.

Reflective writing is not an invitation to throw academic caution to the winds. Introducing an unsupported opinion with *I think/I believe* does not change this essential requirement of academic work – to show the basis for statements you make.

Evidence? What evidence?

If your reader is to see you as a thoughtful, reflective person, your evidence needs to be convincing. It is not sufficient to make statements using buzzwords or assertions about what you have learnt or the insights you have gained. These need to be evidenced too, both from your personal experience and from your related reading.

Read what Jamie wrote. Then check your reactions with ***what a tutor might think.***

A tutor might think: 'Really?? You tell me you have gained cultural competence but you don't show me any evidence that you have or that you know what it is. I don't have any confidence that your practice will change ...

Jamie wrote ...	Tutor's advice ...
After reflecting on this incident I have developed my cultural awareness and my skills in cultural assessment of clients. I feel that I have gained cultural competence as a result of this experience, and will apply this to my future practice ...	***Advice for your redraft:*** *Do some reading – start with Papadopoulos on the concept of cultural competence. Do you believe that anyone can ever be truly 'culturally competent'? How do you feel you could develop your skills, knowledge and attitudes in relation to this aspect of your practice?*

A reflective writer will demonstrate understanding of their sources, and link these to their reflections on their experiences.

See how Jamie has acted on the tutor's advice:

A critical reader might think:
Clear statement of the outcome of Jamie's reflection on the incident. Shows you know how the theory about 'cultural competence' translates into practice.
Not overstated – language reflects the right degree of hesitation.
Points to another source that introduces another factor ...

Some time later ... Jamie's redraft	Tutor feedback might say:
Looking back I can see now why professionals should assess clients' cultural needs – so they can offer culturally sensitive care. I feel that I have gained a degree of 'cultural competence' (Papadopoulos 2006). I would question, however, whether this is possible to achieve completely. Holland and Hogg (2010) point out that the achievement of cultural competence is dependent on practitioners addressing their prejudices. Prejudices are hard to address if you don't know you have them – this is clearly something I need to continue to work on in my future practice …	*You have critically appraised the concept of cultural competence, linking your own experiences and reflections, with different authors' perspectives and interpretations.*

In reflective writing you aim to achieve a balance between your personal perspective, experience and ideas, and the requirements of good academic practice and rigorous thinking. This means:

- having something to say about a topic – a POINT
- or having a perspective, a line of reasoning – an ARGUMENT
- demonstrating that you use EVIDENCE – are well informed, have read, understood and used debates and sources of information
- saying it, in a way that draws together your ideas and experiences, and the ideas and experiences of others – in an appropriate STYLE.

14 Getting the balance right

If you get comments like this …

Is this just your opinion?

This looks like an emotional response without any evidence of a search through the literature …

… you need to shift the balance from **personal opinion** to **evidence** and use more words and phrases like those in Box E!

Box P for Personal … to introduce personal experience	Box E for Evidence … to link to support/evidence
I have had some experience of … *I felt at the time that this was …* *I now understand that …* *I had previously thought that …* *What really stood out for me was …* *I am interested in … because …* *I also think that …* *Personally I found …*	*A study by* Dahl (2007) *showed that …* */ suggests that … / claims that …* Dahl (2007) *proposed that … / argues that* Dahl (2007) *supports this view …* *Based on this framework …* *Research by* the DfES (2007) *indicates that* *An further example of … details how …* (Dahl 2007)

How sure are you?

You don't want to overstate or oversimplify. Issues are rarely simple and something that applies or works well in one context may not in another. A one-size-fits-all approach to ideas or issues gives the impression that you have not understood their complexity and are missing the point. A reflective person will be aware of alternative views, and be careful to convey this in their writing.

If you get comments like …

> *Evidence?*
> *How do you know?*
> *Do other studies show similar patterns?*

> *In ALL cases? This looks like rather a generalisation …*

… think hard about exactly what you do want to say, and pick the right words so that you don't overstate. Try using more phrases like those in Box D than Box C!

Box C for Certainty	**Box D for Doubt** **… a more questioning approach**
It is true to say that … *I knew that …* *I am sure that …*	*It could be the case that …* *The approach taken by* Dahl (2007) *appears to have encouraging results with … although Jones (2009) suggests that in the longer term …* Dahl (2007) *claims that …* *Another interpretation of this is …* *One possibility is that …*

You have to work at choosing the right word or phrase to express the degree of certainty or uncertainty you want to convey. Reflect on it before you write!

For more suggestions for words to use see the Academic Phrasebank: www.phrasebank.manchester.ac.uk/

Part 3 has focused on how to ensure that good reflective writing is also good academic writing. It has shown how to draw together reflections arising from your personal experience on the one hand and from your reading on the other into convincing, well-evidenced reflective writing.

Sometimes you are asked to structure writing in a particular way to encourage you to analyse and reflect on both your personal experience and your reading. Part 4 considers some of these structures.

PART 4 USING FRAMEWORKS IN REFLECTIVE WRITING

Part 4 considers the use of frameworks for reflective writing. A 'framework'[5] offers a structure for thinking and for analysing a problem, situation or experience. It can help you to draw out the learning points from an experience by using a systematic approach:

> *It is not sufficient to have an experience in order to learn. Without reflecting upon this experience it may quickly be forgotten, or its learning potential lost.* (Gibbs 1988 p9)

It's rather like adding a picture frame to a sketch – you can stand back, look at it, reflect on it, and feel that the sketch is now something to be valued.

---

5 For more on frameworks, see *Getting Critical* in this series.

Students who work – or are planning to work – as practitioners in particular fields, such as healthcare, business or education, are often required to present their reflective writing in a particular format, using an established framework. Each model has its own particular strengths and uses.

Four frameworks are outlined in Chapter 15:

1 **Framework for reflective practice** (Rolfe et al. 2001)
2 **Reflection before, during and after action** (Schön 1983)
3 **Experiential learning** (Kolb 1984)
4 **The learning cycle** (Honey and Mumford 1986)

In Chapter 16 **Gibbs' reflective cycle** (1988) is considered in more detail using an extended piece of reflective writing from Health and Social Care.

15 Choosing a framework

Check your guidance so you are clear about the form your reflective writing should take. Are you being asked to:

- *use* a particular framework
- *choose* a framework
- *combine* or *adapt* a framework?

If you have choice or flexibility about the framework you use, you will be expected to explain why you chose that particular framework and not another – to *justify* your choice or adaptations. This process sets in train critical thinking about the frameworks as you work out which best suits your situation.

Framework 1: Framework for reflective practice (Rolfe et al. 2001)

This framework drives your writing by inviting you to respond to three questions: **What? So what? Now what?** The questions are simple – but the answers are … over to you!

What? *Keep this short! Give the reader just enough context to understand what comes next.*	**Outline the situation** Consider what you include: actions, consequences, responses, feelings and problems.
So what? *The most substantial part of your work. Make the link between your personal experience and the knowledge and experience of others.*	**Discuss what you have learnt** Examine what you have learnt about yourself … relationships … others … attitudes … practice … understanding Show why it is important.
Now what? *A short section – next steps or action plan.*	**Identify the implications** What impact could these ideas have on your practice? Or thinking? What do you need to do to improve future outcomes?

Carl used this framework in a short reflection on his practice as a final year student nurse:

What?

A patient in my placement area had an intravenous fluid infusion running; the entry site in his hand had become very sore and inflamed. The cannula was removed and, to my surprise, it was decided that

The incident

the infusion did not need to be replaced. This made me question whether the intravenous infusion could have been stopped sooner, in order to reduce the risks resulting from having a cannula in place.

Carl's reaction and observation

Questioning approach – and evidence of knowledge

So what?

The use of intravenous fluids and of intravenous cannulae should be avoided unless absolutely necessary (Workman 1999; Clayton et al. 1999). Nurses and doctors should therefore constantly assess whether clients need to have intravenous fluids, and they should remove cannulae immediately if they are not required for any other purpose.

Carl steps back and checks his knowledge base from reading

Thoughts about improvements

Now what?

In future I will monitor carefully whether patients need to have intravenous fluids, and I will ensure that I discuss this with my colleagues. I will also make sure that intravenous cannulae are removed

Resolution about future actions

Awareness of interactions with colleagues

immediately if they are no longer required, to prevent secondary complications.

References

Clayton J, Entwistle B, Pickering S and Tune M (1999). Collecting the evidence: Nursing management of intravenous therapy. *Clinical Effectiveness in Nursing*. 3(1) 25–33.

Workman B (1999). Peripheral intravenous therapy management. *Nursing Standard*. 14(4) 53–60.

Framework 2: Reflection before, during and after action (Schön 1983)

The model of reflection suggested by Donald Schön asks the questions: when should we reflect on an action or activity? How does reflection change perspectives before, during and after an experience?

He suggested that the reflective practitioner is reflecting continuously:

Before an experience	During an experience	After an experience
What do you think might happen? *What might be the challenges?* *What do I need to know or do in order to be best prepared for these?*	What's happening now, as you make rapid decisions? *Is it working out as I expected?* *Am I dealing with the challenges well?* *Is there anything I should do, say or think to make the experience successful?* *What am I learning from this?*	What are your insights immediately after, when feelings are still fresh, and/or later when you have more emotional distance from the event? *In retrospect how did it go?* *What did I particularly value and why?* *Is there anything I would do differently before or during a similar experience?* *What have I learnt?*

Below, Joanna used this framework for her account of watching the television series *Seven Up* as part of her course: she notes her thoughts before, during and one semester after the viewing:

Before the experience	During the experience	After the experience
At first I wasn't sure why we would be interested in the story of ordinary people. I wondered why it was part of the module … I thought it would be about the class system and it would show us what happened typically … I also thought that seeing the characters every 7th year all through their lives might be boring and repetitive.	While I was watching, I was amazed how interesting I found the people. I couldn't believe how individual and unique each one was. I felt as I watched that I was really getting to know them. I wasn't bored for a single moment.	In retrospect, I realise just how much I learnt from the series *Seven Up* – the idea from Pavlenko and Lantolf (2000) that people change and 'reorganise' themselves. I understood much better Byram's (1994) ideas of 'savoirs' – ways of understanding the people we tend to stereotype. Also, it made me think again about Stead's article (1989) on how films present class, and whether this too is stereotyped.

Recording her reflections at each point in the experience shows Joanna (and her reader!) how her perspective changed during the course of this experience. She has further enriched the experience by reflecting on the links between the films and her wider reading related to the subjects of social stereotypes, class and individuality.

Framework 3: Experiential learning (Kolb 1984)

Many thinkers and writers about the learning process see learning as cyclical: each time learning takes place it leads to the next phase of learning and the cycle starts again.

In this model, Kolb shows how reflection on an experience leads the individual to form concepts about that experience, and to be able to generalise from one experience to another. From there you move on to the next phase of actively planning how to change what you do next time … and the cycle starts again.

Kolb also identified different types of preferred learning styles. Kolb's ideas and models have since been developed and adapted both by himself and by other theorists – including Honey and Mumford (pp. 87–8) and Gibbs (pp. 90–102).

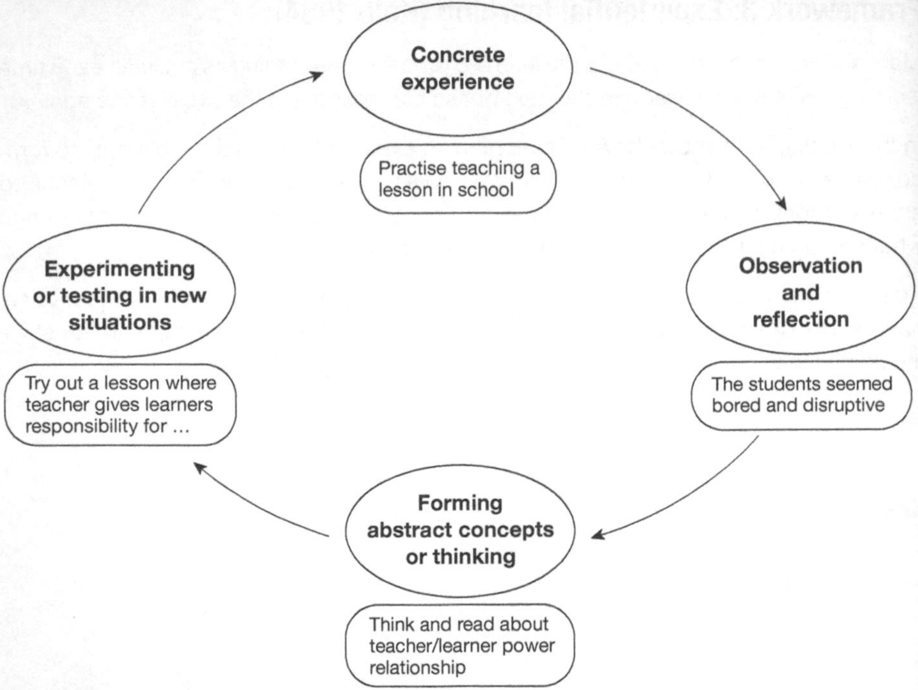

Concrete experience
Practise teaching a lesson in school
Observation and reflection
The students seemed bored and disruptive
Forming abstract concepts or thinking
Think and read about teacher/learner power relationship
Experimenting or testing in new situations
Try out a lesson where teacher gives learners responsibility for ...

Framework 4: The learning cycle (Honey and Mumford 1986)

You can see the short, but distinct, journey from Kolb to Honey and Mumford.

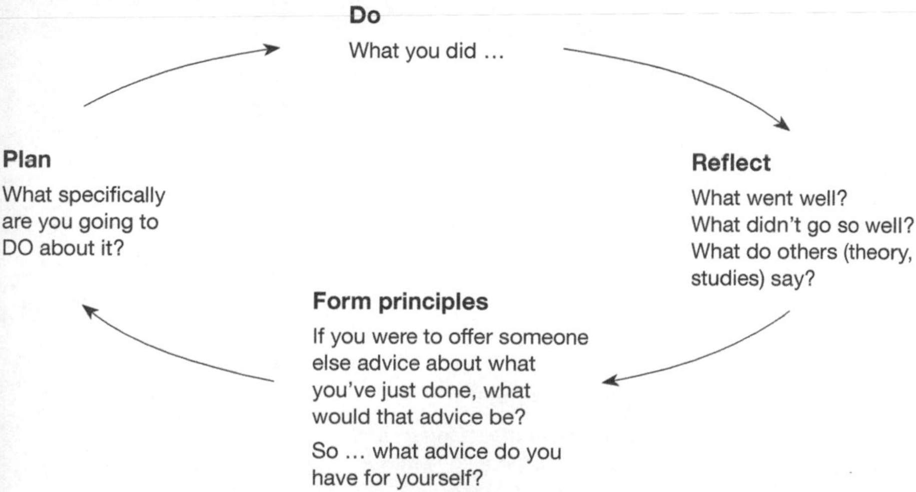

Do
What you did …
Reflect
What went well?
What didn't go so well?
What do others (theory, studies) say?
Form principles
If you were to offer someone else advice about what you've just done, what would that advice be?
So … what advice do you have for yourself?
Plan
What specifically are you going to DO about it?

Ben's (pp. 42–4) reflective journal entry loosely followed this structure. If he had chosen to use it explicitly, he could have organised it like this:

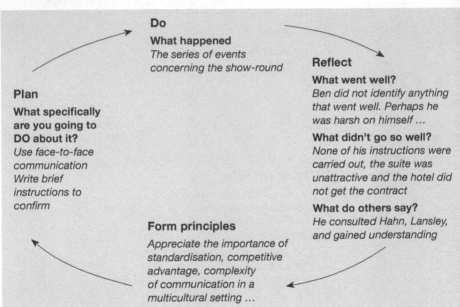

Do

What happened

The series of events concerning the show-round

Reflect

What went well?

Ben did not identify anything that went well. Perhaps he was harsh on himself …

What didn't go so well?

None of his instructions were carried out, the suite was unattractive and the hotel did not get the contract

What do others say?

He consulted Hahn, Lansley, and gained understanding

Form principles

Appreciate the importance of standardisation, competitive advantage, complexity of communication in a multicultural setting …

Plan

What specifically are you going to DO about it?

Use face-to-face communication

Write brief instructions to confirm

Honey and Mumford also developed theories about preferred learning styles (Activist, Reflector, Theorist, Pragmatist) linked to the phases of the learning cycle. Students are sometimes asked to complete this Learning Styles Questionnaire,[6] to reflect on what it tells you about how you learn, and consider how you might extend your range of learning styles. This in itself can be set as a piece of reflective writing.

6 If you google 'Honey and Mumford Learning Styles questionnaire', you may not find the exact questionnaire, but you will find adaptations.

16 Using a framework for reflection: Gibbs' reflective cycle

Graham Gibbs (1988) adapted the experiential learning cycle to acknowledge the importance of feelings and emotion in learning:

> *It is from the feelings and thought emerging from this reflection that generalisations or concepts can be generated. And it is generalisations or concepts that allow new situations to be tackled effectively.* (Gibbs 1988 p9)

He also emphasises the importance of being able to generalise, to transfer knowledge and insights gained from one situation to another. As a result, this framework is frequently used in developing practitioner courses (such as Healthcare and Business).

The reflective cycle

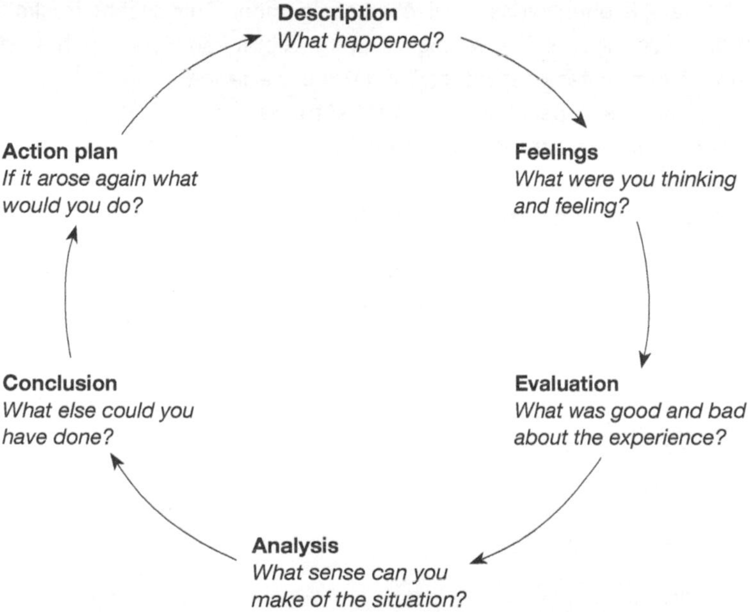
Description
What happened?
Feelings
What were you thinking and feeling?
Evaluation
What was good and bad about the experience?
Analysis
What sense can you make of the situation?
Conclusion
What else could you have done?
Action plan
If it arose again what would you do?

'Reflect on an incident that occurred in your workplace/placement ...'

This sort of task is often set as a reflective assignment. This section tracks the development of a piece of reflective writing using the Gibbs framework, in three steps:

1 An extract from notes briefly describing **the experience**.

2 An analysis of the experience using **Gibbs' model**.

3 A short **reflective report**, ready to hand in.

1 The experience: a Community Practitioner at work

Lin is a Community Practitioner with a varied caseload. She has arranged to visit Martha and her family. Martha (aged 8) has been diagnosed as clinically obese.

Extracts from Lin's notes:

March 3rd Visited Martha and her mum - agreed a plan to help Martha lose weight through diet, food diary, exercise. To review in 6 weeks.

April 12th No weight loss at all. Martha obviously not sticking to plan. Why ever not??? But they seem happy enough to see me again, so - try again ... See if anyone else in the team has any ideas ...

April 20th They did! Read some policy docs by DoH and NAO. Plus an interesting article about a family approach. I guess I need to try more creative approaches ... Strange coincidence - on the TV last night a programme on exercise for overweight kids showed how hard it is to change and sustain change ...

April 28th Set up a family meeting with Martha and her family, fingers crossed the School Nurse can make it ...

2 The model: analysis using Gibbs' reflective cycle

This diagram shows how this experience can be analysed using the phases of Gibbs' reflective cycle:

Action plan
If it arose again what would you do?

Next steps

- Meet school nurse (agree plan)
- Discuss approaches to mealtimes and exercise with Martha and family
- Agree individual plan with Martha and family

In future

- Apply my new knowledge when working with other familes
- Apply for study day on childhood obesity

Get to know Martha and Sonia better … involve them … more creative, family centred approach. Link with other services including school.

Conclusion
What else could you have done?

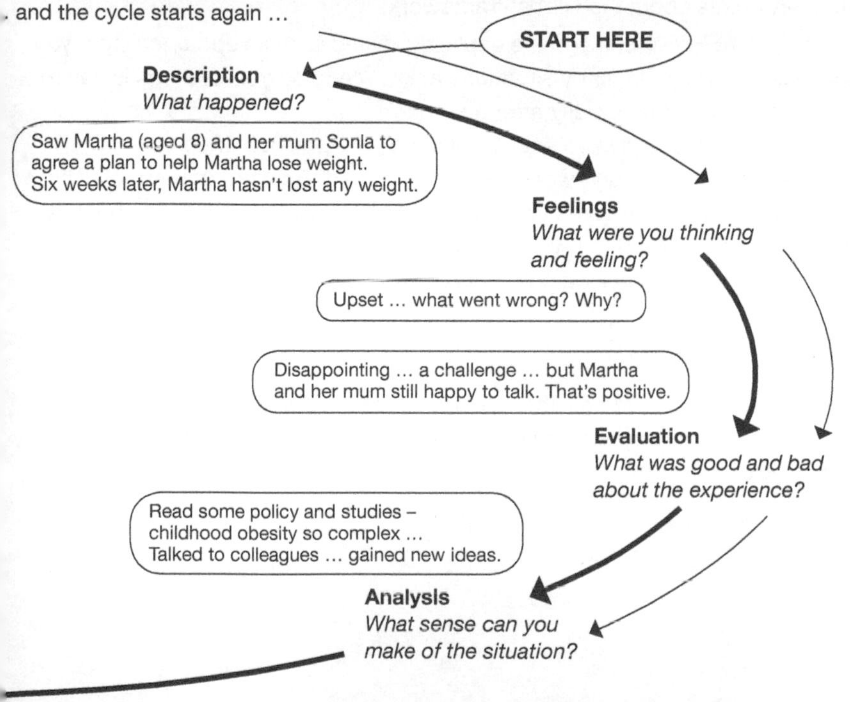

. and the cycle starts again …
START HERE
Description
What happened?
Saw Martha (aged 8) and her mum Sonia to agree a plan to help Martha lose weight. Six weeks later, Martha hasn't lost any weight.
Feelings
What were you thinking and feeling?
Upset … what went wrong? Why?
Disappointing … a challenge … but Martha and her mum still happy to talk. That's positive.
Evaluation
What was good and bad about the experience?
Read some policy and studies – childhood obesity so complex … Talked to colleagues … gained new ideas.
Analysis
What sense can you make of the situation?

Note some key points about the Gibbs' framework:

- Acknowledging FEELINGS. If you are explicitly invited to write about feelings, you are more likely to do so. In many situations acknowledging your feelings is key to being able to move on, especially after a setback.
- The EVALUATION phase. It is so easy to overlook the positive when you are disappointed that things didn't work out as you hoped. Being prompted to add a reflection on 'evaluation' ensures you include the positives as well as the negatives.
- The importance of ANALYSIS – where you draw in all the additional sources of ideas and information in seeking solutions or strategies for your problem.

3 The reflective report

In the final write-up, you can see the full version of Lin's actions and thoughts, the 'value-added' of her reading and discussions, and the power of reflection at every stage of the cycle.

A reflective report on working with a family

Description

After noting that Martha, an 8-year-old girl, had become clinically obese, I arranged to speak to her with her mother, Sonia, to discuss an appropriate dietary plan for Martha to follow. I gave them a food diary to complete, and recommended a programme of gentle exercise to build into Martha's daily routine. Six weeks later, however, Martha's weight had not reduced at all, and they were no longer following our agreed plan.

This section should be brief, but should set out the key points of the incident that you want to reflect upon.

Feelings

I was surprised and upset that my interventions had not been successful. I was disappointed that Martha and her mother hadn't followed my advice, and I was anxious to find a way to help Martha to regain a healthy weight.

Again, this section should generally be brief.

Evaluation

This was a challenging experience. I had not received any specialist training related to obesity in childhood, which limited how much I could help Martha and Sonia. However, on the positive side, they still seemed happy to engage with me, and I felt determined to find a new approach to help them.

This section should provide a balanced appraisal of the situation.

Analysis

This should generally be the most detailed section, in which you link to relevant theory/policy/literature to help you make sense of your experiences and your feelings. In an academic piece this is likely to be even longer and more detailed, linking to a wider range of sources to help you build your discussion and arguments.

It is acknowledged that a variety of factors need to be taken into account when supporting people to make changes to improve their health and lifestyle, including physical, mental, social and environmental issues (Department of Health 2010). An action plan has recently been set out for tackling obesity in all age groups in England (Department of Health 2011), involving a range of services and professionals including schools, health care professionals and other bodies. This document emphasises the importance of local leadership in addressing obesity through a range of strategies including promoting active travel, promoting access to healthy food choices, and promoting access to opportunities for physical activity.

It is argued that a creative, child- and family-centred approach should be taken (Wild 2006; National Audit Office 2006) to support families in changing their lifestyles. There are many resources that can be used to support them, for example the 'Change4Life' initiative (National Health Service 2011), through which all members of a family can be supported to aim towards a more healthy lifestyle, by making changes to their dietary and exercise habits.

In this section Lin is linking to policy and theory to help her to analyse the issues she has faced in her practice. This will help her to make sense of her experiences and learn from them. Her writing demonstrates transformative learning, which will influence her future practice.

Conclusion

After discussing this incident with my colleagues, and reading a range of policy and literature on the topic, I have realised that childhood obesity is a complex issue and that a 'one size fits all' approach to supporting children and their families is not appropriate. Looking back on this incident, I can

This indicates that Lin has learnt from her research and her reflections, and that her knowledge and perspectives have changed. She will be able to apply this to develop her practice in the future.

now see that I should have spent more time getting to know Martha and her mother, and that a more individualised, family-centred approach rather than a 'prescriptive' approach would have been more effective.

I have become aware that effective communication is essential between all those who may be involved in supporting a child to lose weight – the child, their family and professionals.

In this section Lin sums up the lessons she has learned from reflecting on this incident, demonstrating how the learning will influence her future practice.

Action plan

After reflecting on this incident, I will now apply a wider range of strategies to support children like Martha. I will work alongside colleagues in the community and in schools to ensure that children and their families are provided with appropriate education and support to meet their individual needs. I will continue to discuss issues such as this with my colleagues to help me to develop my skills and knowledge. I plan to find out more about childhood

Here Lin sums up, giving a clear plan for how she will change her practice in the long term and short term as a result of what she has learned from her reflections.

obesity, thereby enhancing my knowledge and my practice – including attending a formal study day on childhood obesity.

References

Department of Health (2010). *Healthy Lives, Healthy People: Our Strategy for Public Health in England*. London: Department of Health.

Department of Health (2011). *Healthy Lives, Healthy People: A Call to Action on Obesity in England*. London: Department of Health.

National Audit Office (2006). *Tackling Child Obesity – First Steps*. London: Her Majesty's Stationery Office.

National Health Service (2011). *Change4Life for Families*. Available at: http://www.nhs.uk/Change4Life/Pages/change-for-life-families.aspx (accessed 29/10/11).

Wild S (2006). Taking a family approach to childhood obesity. *Independent Nurse*. 23 Oct. 23, pp 42–4.

Here Lin provides references so that her reader can find the documents she refers to in her work.

THE END … or is it? This may be the conclusion of your reflections on a single learning experience, but it lies at the heart of your development as a professional. What happens next time you are in a similar situation? You can continue to use Gibbs' reflective cycle to chart your ongoing learning and development.

....

The use of a framework for reflection helps the writer to focus on the change and development needed to become a more effective practitioner in just about any work setting. Writing of this sort is often used as part of a work placement portfolio, where the focus on outcomes is a useful rehearsal for the next stage – taking the step into the world of employment.

Part 5 considers the importance of reflection in this next step.

PART 5

REFLECTION FOR CAREER PLANNING

To be convincing in the graduate market you have to master the skill of reflection. Employers are genuinely interested in who you are …
Careers Adviser

Part 5 is designed to remind you that reflection is a habit for life and is particularly important in preparing for the next step – into employment. This part includes practical 'workshops' to help you with this reflection.

Just as a close reading of course materials tells you what academic staff are looking for in your writing, employers tell you what they are looking for in:

- the *job description* (JD) – what you have to be able to **do**
- the *person requirements* (PR) (or *person specification*, PS) – the sort of person you have to **be**
- the additional information you need to take on board about the organisation – on their website as well as in the applicant information.

There are, however, differences: an employer is less interested in what you know and how you know it than in what you can do and who you are.

An employer looking at an application will be asking:

- **What can you do?** What are you good at? … *to see how you match the JD*
- **What do you want**? What do you enjoy? … *to understand your motivation*
- **Who are you?** … *to see how you match the PS*.

Your application must provide the answers to these questions. To do this **you** need to know what they are, and to have done your groundwork in advance. Time for some hard thinking and reflection …

17 Doing the groundwork

The workshops in this section are designed to help you get started on this reflection.

Workshop 1: What's your story?

Give yourself 15 minutes.

Look back over the past 10 years and map out what you've done.

→ Take a large sheet of paper – A3 is ideal.
→ Put yourself near the top: today.
→ Put yourself at the bottom – 10 years ago.
→ Sketch the journey in between.
→ On the left of the pathway mark in the experiences that have been important for you.
→ On the right, jot down what you learnt from these experiences.
→ At the very top, jot down three possible directions you might go in the future.

Why do this?

- It's the outline of a 'convincing narrative': Where am I? How did I get here? Where am I going?
- It's not just a record of what you've done (education, work, study) but also your personal account, evaluations and feelings about these experiences.
- You can add to it over time or use it as a basis for discussions about your future plans.

For Workshop 2 you need an advertisement for a job you would consider applying for. If you don't have one handy, see
www.prospects.ac.uk/
http://targetjobs.co.uk/

Workshop 2: Can you do it? Matching the job description

Look carefully at the job description of the job you have identified. For each item ask yourself:

→ Can I do it? Yes? No? Maybe?
→ Cross out the definite 'No' items.

[Choose another ad if you need to, and repeat …]

When you have 'Yes' or 'Maybe' against all the 'Essentials' in the list, ask yourself:

→ How can I show that I can? What specific experience can I point to? Don't be too harsh on yourself. Employers know that recent graduates will have limited experience. Think that little bit harder about examples you can use.

→ How might you be able to turn a 'Maybe' into a 'Yes'? If you have a gap, what are you prepared to do to address it?

Why do this?

It helps you to:

- focus on exactly what a JD is asking for – through close analysis
- think positively about what you can or could do
- reflect on how to persuade an employer that you can do it by pointing to the right sort of evidence …

Workshop 3: I'm good at …

Don't be shy about saying what you're good at. It's only embarrassing if you have no evidence or examples to support what you are saying. This workshop is designed to help you start finding that evidence.

It feels so weird to say 'I'm really good at …' It seems so melodramatic, blowing my own trumpet. (Student)

If you get the chance, ask a friend to do the workshop at the same time.

Jot down one thing you enjoy doing, and one thing you are good at …

	I enjoy …	**I'm good at …**
At home, with friends or family		
At college/university		
At work, work placement or in other aspects of your life		

Give yourself 5 minutes.

If you did this at the same time as a friend

→ ask them to guess what you wrote

→ you guess what they wrote.

And discuss!

I believe in the benefits of outdoor learning ... I played football semi-professionally ... I work with the youth coaching team.

I enjoy the fact that each day is different ...

There are several things I'd change, but I'm happy the CD I created will help new starters ...

I know that I can make a difference and for me this is important ...

I have a particular interest in cross-curricular uses of drama ...

Why do this?

- It helps you demonstrate what you're good at and what you enjoy and helps you to make statements about your strengths without embarrassment or fear of overstating.
- It ensures you *analyse* your strengths and avoid *describing* incidents (which tends to be too long, and boring to read).
- It is about YOU. Plenty of people have done xyz, but no one will have precisely your take on it or way of expressing it – personal but not private writing.

Applying for jobs is about convincing someone – a potential employer – that you are the person that matches what they are looking for. Finding the right evidence is reassuring and convincing for the reader.

You're not like the embarrassing contestants in a talent show ...

You have **EVIDENCE**!!

18 Finding your evidence

Meeting the 'person specification' (or 'requirements')

In a 'person specification' an employer explains who they are looking for. For example, they may be looking for someone who can …

stay calm under pressure … be well organised … meet tight deadlines … has good interpersonal skills …

And who

… has a genuine interest in … is a good team player … has good IT skills … enthusiasm for … good work ethic …

In an application you have to make that match between the qualities, skills and experience they are looking for, and the qualities, skills and experience you have – your EVIDENCE. Through examples you justify your claims.

…ur skills and personal …lities	And how you can evidence this …
I can deal with pressure … stay calm	I worked in a busy hotel reception …
I can work to deadlines	I handed in all my assignments on time, with two kids and a part-time job …
I have good customer service skills	I worked part-time for M&S and undertook customer service training …
I have an excellent record of getting the job done well and on time	… based on service user and management feedback systems …
I have good analytical skills	I analysed data on [travel] trends from company websites, trade and academic journals for a 500 word report
In the office I created an enthusiastic, cohesive, positive vibe	… highlighted by my manager

Oh yeah? Everyone says that …

OK. Yes, being calm here is important

Yes, that's in the Person Spec

Impressive …

Included just because it's in the PS?

Must have shown promise for the company to train …

Your skills and personal qualities	And how you can evidence this ...
I believe a positive and stimulating classroom is essential …	… to make Maths fun I introduced Venn diagrams by asking children to sort dolls' laundry into the correct 'washing basket' …
Over to you ...	

As you read these, you can see the person writing it. Using evidence well helps you to write about yourself (*I*, *me*, *my*) in your own 'voice'. If what you've just written doesn't sound right to you, you can be sure it won't sound right to anyone else!

Students often seem to think they have to be somebody they aren't – a cardboard cutout of an ideal applicant. (Careers Adviser)

A notebook (or folder, or e-portfolio or personal development plan) can be handy to record your examples and thoughts. Little achievements that you take for granted can – when you reflect on it – provide you with just the detail you need to support a quality you want to evidence.

Be as specific as you can – when, where, the context – it makes it real for the reader. (Lecturer, Healthcare)

Writing focus: the right kind of evidence?

You need to supply the right kind of evidence for your reader.

For **lecturers** your sources (references) are the evidence of your ability to link your reflections on your personal experiences with research:

Lansley (2000) identifies standardisation as a key hospitality concept … Hahn argues that face-to-face communication as the most effective …
(see Ben's journal pp. 42–4)

Most **employers** want to see examples of **learning in action**, the **outcome** of reflection:

I realised that face-to-face communication is the most effective in … [it] resulted in a booking …
(see Ben's STAR statement p. 119)

Ben's reflection on the outcomes of his personal experience is the right sort of evidence for an employer – not the academic references he used in his placement portfolio.

The wrong kind of evidence

Employers often give helpful advice on how to make the most of your experience in an application. They know that mature applicants may be changing direction and that younger applicants may have limited work experience. So they encourage you to look at the skills you have developed in the course of your studies.

Here is guidance offered by one employer, explaining some of the qualities they are looking for, in order to help you demonstrate the skills they are seeking.

The skills	The guidance to skill 4
Are you ... the one who can ...	
1 *Coach and develop yourself and others?*	
2 *Communicate with impact and empathy?*	... the better you can support, lead and get along with others, the better you'll get on ... You could have picked up the skills to do this in a number of ways ... as part of a sports team, club or society. Or you might have tackled a course-related project as part of a group or fitted into a new team at work ...
3 *Be curious: learn, share and innovate?*	
4 *Lead and reinforce team success?*	
5 *Build and maintain relationships?*	

Think about the more subtle aspects of leadership – 'support' ' get along'.

How did you pick up these skills? What's your example?

As part of your course, from your involvement in student life or at work? What YOU achieved (not just what 'our team' achieved).

PricewaterhouseCoopers (2011)

Workshop 4: Think of a time when you …

Pick one of the five skill areas listed on the previous page.

→ Take a sheet of A4 paper and fold it into quarters.

→ Put the headings in each of the four corners.

→ Write one of the five skill areas in the middle.

→ Reflect – to pull out the details from the incident under the (relevant) prompts in each quarter.

Start here

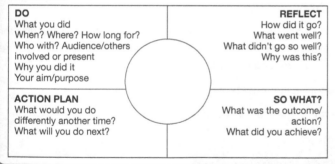

DO What you did When? Where? How long for? Who with? Audience/others involved or present Why you did it Your aim/purpose	**REFLECT** How did it go? What went well? What didn't go so well? Why was this?
ACTION PLAN What would you do differently another time? What will you do next?	**SO WHAT?** What was the outcome/ action? What did you achieve?

Source: Adapted from a *Future Leaders* workshop activity, with thanks to Dan Ferrett, Careers Adviser, Oxford Brookes University.

You now have an analysis of an example you can use in writing or talking about your skills and experiences – a 'transferable skill' that shows you could deal with a different situation, an addition to your 'store' of examples.

It could be useful to run this exercise several times. Include one incident that didn't go so well initially. Don't airbrush out the difficulties: instead show how you turned it around or learnt from it.

Now for the writing …

Showing your evidence

The STAR technique (Situation, Task, Action, Result) offers a simple structure for *showing* your reader what your skills are. You're not making pompous claims – you're offering a window on who you are and how you do things.

It can be adapted to use for trickier questions:

> *Describe a problem you've recently had to solve*

The STAR framework	Ben's incident (pp. 42–4):	How might you answer this question?
SITUATION What happened? (Keep it very short.)	As duty manager at [hotel] I was responsible for a VIP show-round on my shift.	
TASK What did you have to do?	My task was to secure a booking for a corporate client by ensuring the rooms were prepared to a high standard. This was not done, and we lost the booking.	
ACTION What did you do to solve the problem? Reflect back to find the right level of detail.	I identified a series of faults with my actions. I researched communication with an international staff group and realised that face-to-face communication and brief written instructions are the most effective.	
RESULT What was the outcome? Make sure you explain what you learnt and what you'd do differently another time.	In preparation for a show-round of a major corporate client the following week, I wrote down and talked through clear instructions for the preparation of the suite (flowers, lighting, bathrobes). I checked an hour in advance. The client was impressed and the show-round resulted in a booking …	

When you string together your statements S-T-A-R, you have a basic, purposeful narrative. Edit it and check that it directly addresses the skills required by the job or the question on the application form and that it has the right level of detail.

So ... *reflect on this* ...
What can you do? What are you good at?
What do you want? What do you enjoy?
Who are you?

If you can do the hard reflection involved in answering these questions, you'll be well prepared for the crucial question:

Good luck!

19 Conclusion: the habit of reflection

We commented earlier (p. 54) that reflection isn't just a one-off activity to complete a task, but can become 'a habit of mind, one that transforms' (Yancey 1998 p12).

Transformation is what education and learning are about. Many people look back on the person they were when they started their course and are struck by how much they have changed. On the surface you're the same person, doing much the same sort of things, but inside, you know you have changed … you've learnt to see or do things differently.

When you write reflectively, you are putting this deeper understanding into words. Let's hope your reader will see it too, and tell you in their feedback:

I am really impressed with the depth of your knowledge and understanding. You are reflective, and while you are enthusiastic about […] you show you understand the difficulties …

References

Entwhistle N (2009). *Teaching for understanding at university: deep approaches and distinctive ways of thinking.* Basingstoke: Palgrave Macmillan.

Gibbs G (1988). *Learning by doing: a guide to teaching and learning methods.* Oxford: Further Education Unit, Oxford Polytechnic.

Honey P and Mumford A (1986). In Mumford A *Effective learning.* London: IPD.

Kolb DA (1984). *Experiential learning: experience as the source of learning and development.* Englewood Cliffs, NJ: Prentice Hall.

Moon J (2005). *Learning through reflection. Guide for busy academics No 4.* York: The Higher Education Academy.

PricewaterhouseCoopers (no date). *Employability guide*. Available at: www.pwc.com/uk/en/careers/documents/student/pwc-employability-2011.pdf [Accessed 26 November 2011].

Rolfe G, Freshwater D and Jasper M (2001). *Critical reflection for nursing and the helping professions: a user's guide*. Basingstoke: Palgrave Macmillan.

Schön, D (1983). *The reflective practitioner: how professionals think in action*. New York: Basic Books.

Williams K (2009). *Getting critical*. Basingstoke: Palgrave Macmillan.

Williams K, Bethell E, Lawton J, Parfitt-Brown C, Richardson M and Rowe V (2011). *Completing your PhD*. Basingstoke: Palgrave Macmillan.

Yancey KC (1998). *Reflection in the writing classroom.* Logan, UT: Utah State University Press.

Index